Appendices Pulled
from a Study on Light

Geoffrey Babbitt

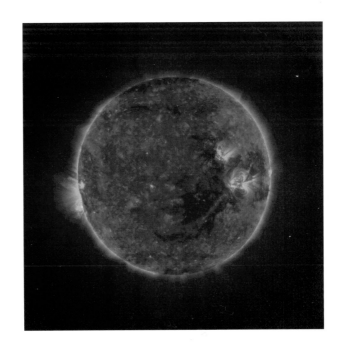

SPUYTEN DUYVIL
New York City

Acknowledgments

The poems and essay below first appeared (sometimes in earlier versions) in the following journals.

The Bacon Review: "Image on the Edge," "So It Says Today," & "Song for Menalcas"

Barnwood Magazine: "The Brush Reminds Paint of Itself"

Barrow Street: "Vespers: to Kathryn"

BlazeVOX: "Bottleneck, Bottle Glass," "Toward a Compass Rose," "Breaches," & "Latitude, Stratum"

The Collagist: "In the Gloom, the Gold Gathers the Light Against It"

CutBank: "Prime: No Note"

DIAGRAM: "*Proem*: Rare Halo" (as "Parhelion")

Free Verse: "We Wend Our Way Across Two Imaginings and Find the World Is Real"

Greatcoat: "Kamares at Sundown" & "All Within Eyeshot"

Improbable Object: "Which Is Raising Its Little Hand"

Notre Dame Review: "Ad Laudes," "Christmas Morning Matins," & "Coda"

Redactions: "Ad Tertiam"

Washington Square: "Ad Matutinas de Sancto Spiritu"

Western Humanities Review: "Rest Where Streams," "All Along Reservoir Road," "Eye Out of the Air," & "Lux Perpétua Lúceat Eis: Those Paws Buckle Under"

Witness: "The Writer over the Page Is Driven Down But Like a Robin by a Worm"

Word For/Word: "An Own Place," "Codex," "Kalends," "Bottom Left Corner of Litany of Saints," "Office of the Dead," & "De Sanctissima Trinitate"

Library of Congress Cataloging-in-Publication Data

Names: Babbitt, Geoffrey, author.
Title: Appendices pulled from a study on light / Geoffrey Babbitt.
Description: New York City : Spuyten Duyvil, [2018]
Identifiers: LCCN 2017038606 | ISBN 9781944682897
Classification: LCC PS3602.A224 A6 2018 | DDC 811/.6--dc23
LC record available at https://lccn.loc.gov/2017038606

for Charles O. Hartman

Contents

PROEM: RARE HALO

A need to arc is where it starts.
As in the arc of morning light,
A halo above the first frost clinging
      to the grass,
Above the hoary shadow's shape the garage casts,
      above the garage.

A halo leaves no story.
A halo becomes the arc it needs.
      The arc of telling
grants death once begun,
      which it perpetually begins.

A need to arc is where it starts.
Morning light *pinwheeled in a sparrow's*
      //// eye, for instance.
Any arc is a form of play,
      and light is always open.

A halo above the first frost,
Light strikes the blue garage,
      and the light opens out.
A need to arc is under way.
Which goes right through us.

After one has abandoned a belief in God,
poetry is that essence which takes its place as life's redemption.
—Wallace Stevens

I call poetry factual telepathy.
—Susan Howe

CODEX

strewn foliate border:
       a trace of
the arc of the page—a form
of play, of prayer
fire-calling away—
       we are idle
and so are our flowers—

τόπος means
gods from untilled earth
       —the sun
unlocks light the text
had socked in

a trace unnameable—place
holding the child
to the first frost,
the street lamp, the pasture—

It's redundant to say heaven is without margins.

When the mind knows a place, the sense perceptions it can elicit become familiar on a level beneath reflective awareness. Known intimately enough, any particular can be as unthought of as one's own heartbeat.

The wooden sign that Rev. Hightower once worked bits of broken glass into so it'd glitter under the street lamp becomes, over time, a familiar low oblong shape without any significance at all, low at the street end of the shallow lawn. Unremembered because known.

Before knowledge evinces itself through forgetting, perceptions flood. Attention holds them up to light, and the light is always changing. The eye passively receives, or else it reaches.

But the senses do not go all the way. Beyond them Neptune shakes the walls and Little Infants creep out of the flowery mould into green fields.

There is an unnameable other side to what a place's name or description can designate.

The plot is collaboration.

MATINS: BOTTLENECK, BOTTLE GLASS

blue glass, green glass, shell sanded,
gritty shine—island
slips into sea—light spilled by the sun
is skinwine—seven degrees
of azure: sea, sea, sky, dome, sky, trimming,
sky—seen from the oleanders
the beach is a ring, the sea
a lake—sun scrubs white things whiter—each schist
has two faces—one
up, one down—the highest hill's
made of burning faces—now is
a good time to build a bridge—we go

IN THE GLOOM, THE GOLD GATHERS THE LIGHT AGAINST IT

I don't know why I am drawn to illuminated manuscripts.

I remember walking through a book when I was young. An entire medieval manuscript, a Book of Hours, was unbound, quires unsewn, each bifolium displayed in a brightly lit glass box. Dozens of these luminous cases were in a huge, marmoreal exhibition room. The displays had magnifying glasses, and I remember someone pointing out dark speckles on a sheet of parchment that were traces of the calf's or sheep's hair follicles. There was a blue that was the deepest blue I had ever seen—ultramarine on Mary's robes, inside a golden initial, spread across the page as sky. Glistening gold bands looked like molten scraps of sun. I remember wanting to touch the pages, wanting, for some reason, to put my lips to them.

•

Some manuscripts have legends that are nearly as fascinating as the books themselves. My favorite goes back to sixth century Ireland, and concerns a psalter known as The Cathach of St. Columba. Although the psalter bears the name of St. Columba, it is actually named after the copy Columba made of a manuscript that had been loaned to him by St. Finnian. And therein lies the scandal.

St. Finnian had recently returned from Rome, where the Pope himself had given Finnian a new, superior Latin translation of the Psalms. Because Finnian was friends with Columba and admired his scholarship, the older saint let the younger one borrow it. The new book gripped Columba intensely as he read it, so he copied it without Finnian's permission.

Just before Columba had finished his clandestine task, a messenger sent by Finnian to collect the psalter arrived at St. Columba's church.

The messenger, a young boy, peered into the church through a keyhole and witnessed a miracle. The five fingers on St. Columba's hand were like long candle flames, and from them emanated bright beams that filled the church with light.

The Book of Hours is the book *par excellence*. Because it was practical to own—unlike the Bible, say, which was usually multivoluminous & required a clerical intermediary— the Book of Hours became ubiquitous, thus dubbed "the first best-seller." If many late medieval households owned a single book at all, it would've been a Book of Hours. Since they were for laity, they had a democratizing effect. (As our age has claimed of the Internet).

"You acquire a book with marginalia—a message to an unknown fellow reader, like a letter in a bottle. What next?" —H.J. Jackson

True to Stevens' epigraph, I traded my Catholicism for poetry.

My "I" drops off, slips out of the central text.

The transition from scroll to codex was as momentous as our supplementation of physical books with electronic texts. Some digital texts resemble illuminated manuscripts but only superficially, only in their hypermediacy. They lack manuscripts' most essential quality: their bookness.

As Columba luminously transcribed, his crane—not an uncommon pet for monks of the time—thrust his beak through the keyhole, plucking out the eye of the young voyeur. Blood leaked from his dark orbital socket. The eyeball—legend has it— dangled on his cheek.

The boy went crying to St. Finnian, who performed his own miracle and restored the boy's eye.

St. Finnian was so angry at St. Columba for his textual thievery that their dispute eventually culminated in the Battle of Cúl Drebene in 561 (*cathach* means "battler"). Many men were killed in the battle, and Adomnán of Iona tells us that St. Columba was excommunicated for his role in it. Columba left Ireland.

Some sources say that he exiled himself as atonement for the battle and went on a mission to Scotland, converting the Picts. It was his goal to save more lives than had been lost in battle.

Columba might have used The Cathach of St. Columba as a conversion tool.

Books of Hours developed out of the psalter, which is why they often house the Penitential Psalms (6, 32, 38, 51, 102, 130 & 143) and the Gradual Psalms (120-134).

King David wrote (most of) the Psalms. Or so they say.

As the elder authority who is displaced by a young rising star, St. Finnian's analogue is King Saul, while St. Columba's is King David.

Sure, another copy ruins Finnian's monopolistic stronghold of the new translation in Ireland. But that's from a market perspective, wherein scripture is religious currency. They're both monks who have the same endgame of conversion and spreading the word. So why the feud? Textual possessiveness only goes so far to explain Finnian's drastic reaction to Columba.

How could Columba have redeemed the deaths of 3,000 people? How are these two men considered saints?

On Time and the Office of the Dead

"it is time which is at the heart of Christianity"
—Charles Olson

eight canonical hours	
in a day—ere	
mechanical clock, time	matins
in natural phenomena—	
a girl holding	lauds
light—metaphor	
waiting for a mouth	
—time as emanation	prime
—tangible, integral—	
cyclical hours within	
same plane—minutiae	terce
slipping into light—auras	
unpinnable—	
	sext
the temporal unfolding	
an expression of eternality	
—sun thrashing—	
Office of the Dead reminds medieval believers	none
to prepare—the here	
and now should be put to good	
use—the plot is	vespers
acknowledging the way—nature folded	
into grace, the grace	compline
of something unnameable	

long after the road is a ruin,
cicadas praise its abandonment—
shadows lengthen
to the garden's edge—grapevine,
swollen bunches—bursts from a flower
never before seen—and in the olive
tree—a figure (affinitive?) spills water
into water, pooling close enough to sea
to trickle into—so the sea carries on—
carries farther from road and garden—the figure

she gives her hand to a poppy—blue
currents pay no mind—and not in
this direction only—where else
does a mast's sentinel look away from? and from
what angle comes this
little constellation, this bright bird

KALENDS

Codex: Book of Hours of the Virgin — Date: ca. 1500 — Origin: France
— Use: Rome — Current Location: Toledo Museum of Art — Materials:
Ink, tempera, and brushed or burnished gold on vellum — Binding:
18th c. binding in red morocco with metal clasps — Size: 5 3/16 in.
x 3 7/16 in. — Section: Calendar — Page: 2 verso and 3 recto — Il-
lustration: Pisces, two fish in a lake and fisherman; Aries, the ram
(detail) — Artist: Master of Morgan 85

late 15th century French Book of Hours—
Kalends, gilded "KL" in a brick-red, two-line-tall box
important feasts rubricated—hence "red-letter days"
labors of the month above the calendar, zodiac sign scene below

Februarius: a peasant warming his feet by fire, another bringing in wood—
      a man fishing for two fish in a lake
Maius: rider with his lady on horseback, two attendants—twins with a shield
Augustus: three men thrashing wheat—two virgins holding staffs of wheat
September: a man bringing a full basket to another treading grapes—a girl holding
      scales

and so forth

Books of Hours have a bent for the pastoral

even foliate bar borders can conjure an elsewhere

sprays of acanthus—stylized fleshy fronds—delicate rinceaux—ivy—in Virgil's fourth eclogue's prophecy of the Golden Age's return, nature pays spontaneous homage to the messianic child by abundantly producing acanthus and ivy

in Flemish books, strewn borders tempt the reader to pick flora up off the page

in order to discuss preferences with the bookshop keeper, a customer wanting to commission a Book of Hours might open a second-hand manuscript to a rural scene very different from the bookshop's urban setting

illuminations transport

§

Language and light share the divine.

Medieval believers recited Genesis 1:3 in their sleep: "God said, 'Let there be light,' and there was light."

God's speech act makes light and thereby introduces order. Or as Harold Bloom puts it, "God teaches Himself His own Name, and so begins creation."

Augustine openly reflects on the beginning of the Gospel of John: "You call us, therefore, to understand the Word, God who is with you God... That word is spoken eternally, and by it all things are uttered eternally... You do not cause it to exist other than by speaking."

Scholia and glosses are evidence that texts not only illuminate but also obscure.

"The use of books of Hours by lay people in the late Middle Ages is indeed an aspect of the promotion of lay interiority, the personalizing of religion.... The Book of Hours... offered lay people a share in what was essentially a monastic form of piety." —Eamon Duffy

I attended Catholic school until college. When I was thirteen, my class visited The Monastery of the Ascension, a Benedictine abbey.

Despite living as part of a community, a monk is an isolato.

The margin is a cloister.

"'Gloss' (from the Greek for 'tongue') originally referred to a foreign or obscure word that required explanation; eventually the explanation itself became the gloss (as the most difficult words in poems eventually came to be regarded, by critics, as the keys to interpretation). The degeneration of the word into 'glossing over'—a sophistical explaining away—was abetted by confusion with another word, the glossy gaze that stands for superficial luster. This etymology reflects the modern suspicion of glossing in general." —Lawrence Lipking

As author of Psalms, King David's treatment of light only solidifies his status as St. Columba's analogue.

God's speech creating light prefigures incarnation: sound (the Word) transformed into matter (flesh).

The Psalms say, "The commands of the Lord are radiant, / giving light to the eyes."

John's gospel says, "the Word was God."

The First Letter of John says, "God is light."

How can one ever truly own a religious text? Moreover, why does Columba's copying always overshadow the warfare? Every retelling of this story privileges textual theft over the literal violence of the battle. 3,000 individual lives lost. We prize the symbolic over the literal.

St. Benedict added the eighth and final hour, Compline, to the Liturgical Hours. He is often credited with arranging the Hours. For the Order of St. Benedict, the work portion of the *ora et labora* motto was carried out most predominately through their commitment to writing, which they devoutly undertook in specially designated rooms called *scriptoria*.

"the flame / is solitary and splendid in its upright judgment" —Aimé Césaire

Song for Menalcas

A shepherd sings
into the cave of origins.

On the cave's eave,
birds behave birdily. The cave

is a mouth incapable
of its own tongue.

One bird feeds where the shepherd
has kneeled. Unlike the birds, or the sheep,

the shepherd lives on a table
where no crumb falls—and yet,

a thresher in one shoulder,
in the other a winnower. He lights his pipe

from a twig dipped in the coals of his fire. The birds,
which were beggars at his feet,

become paper—lily white,
dancing around a roseate flame.

The origins are flailed thin, flaked
into ash, scattered by wing beats.

man in a tall pipe
showering under new light—someone stands
in the first place a second time
and wakes to morning light
through the interstices of wet boughs—
fissures in—the seamless
can be cracked wide—here is where
we enter—rain shadow mess
halos—follow into another
—silver breath increases itself—we get in
water to see through surface
from the other side

One can say St. Columba's copying is unethical.

He acts without St. Finnian's permission, and the act of copying destroys the psalter's value, which lay in its uniqueness to Ireland. Retelling the story for its basic impact, an essay on literary property in a 1908 issue of *The Michigan Law Review* finds Columba in the wrong, ending its rendition with the king's memorable decision: "To every cow her calf; to every book its copy." And so the crown sides with Finnian.

And yet, divine light accompanies Columba because God sanctions the saint as he works.

So regardless of whether he commits a transgression, what he does is endorsed by divine will and is, therefore, righteous. The ground we have strayed onto is close to Kierkegaard's "teleological suspension of the ethical." That is, just as Abraham oversteps ethical restrictions when he binds Isaac to the sacrificial altar, so too St. Columba places his telos altogether higher than the ethical realm—instead, in the absolute, in what pleases God.

Morality trumps ethics.

Abraham's justification of sacrificing Isaac is the same used by zealots, extremists, and terrorists who kill for a "holy" cause.

God, according to his Christian definition, transcends ethics and cannot be immoral since his will cannot be anything other than holy.

Of course the king sided with Finnian! (Our King Saul figure.) Every king embodies the anxiety of retention.

In search of knowledge, the Norse god Odin sent his two ravens to survey the world each day. Each night, they reported back. But still, the god wanted to know more. So in exchange for a drink from Mimir's magical well of knowledge, Odin plucked out an eye and tossed it into the well.

After my grandfather had died, I learned to fly fish with some of his old flies. When I found his creel in the extended family's bunkhouse of our old cabin, I didn't *steal* it. I thought of it as rightfully claiming my heritage.

•

The battle duplicates morality's supersession of ethics. Wrong to copy, wrong to kill—unless backed by divine will.

God can thus wipe out as many people as he sees fit. Or have as many eyes as he likes plucked from the sockets of helpless boys.

"Morality is brain damage." —Arthur Rimbaud

Now consider the messenger boy.

Although he is right to follow his master's instructions dutifully, he is, in some larger sense, wrong for intruding upon a miracle. His punishment strikes us as fair and unfair because it is both—thus must he suffer the loss of an eye but also have it restored.

In a sixteenth century version of the Cathach story, the loss of the boy's eye is not the result of a crane's whim but God's decree. Columba gives permission to the crane to pluck out the young boy's eye, so long as God does not object.

God does not.

In some versions, Odin's raven removes his eye.

When Odin wanted to know even more, he pursued the secret runes.

In order to get certain texts or to get just the right bit of knowledge, history has shown that we will go to drastic lengths.

mind briar while bounding
through the underbrush
    —vert chirps—hunting
the trail, the green—each gives way to

    code: *in die illa treménda*
outlaw dogtrout: call the nurse, prepare the shot.
vomit—scrawl change, collect
alms. alms. arms and arms.
rage now, dogtrout! rage

roll on, roll on to the asphodels—
light, give way to, give way to—
dogtrout running through the asphodels

shades can loosen tears onto asphodels;
foot joy over flower—
when dogtrout died I kissed his ear.
ears. each. each.

OFFICE OF THE DEAD

Codex: Officium Beatae Mariae Virginis, made for Pope Leo X, bearing his name and the Medici arms (Leo X was formerly Giovanni di Lorenzo de' Medici) — Date: ca. 1513-1521 — Illustration: Details (see below) — Origin: Northern Italy — Current Location: Toledo Museum of Art — Materials: Ink, tempera, and burnished gold on vellum — Binding: Green velvet with metal clasps — Size: 5 7/16 in. x 3 3/4 in.

The Office of the Dead is one of the final sections in a Book of Hours, usually coming directly before the Suffrages of the Saints, which tends to be last. In Pope Leo X's, however, it is prioritized in an uncharacteristic position near the forefront—coming second, directly after the liturgy for the Office of Matins on Christmas.

An illustration of Lazarus often decorates the verso before the Office begins on the opposite recto. Here, Pope Leo X's name is on a decorative shield beneath Lazarus—as if Leo identifies with Lazarus as Death casts his eyeless stare across the abysmal gutter.

green velvet binding
with metal clasp—a garment
for wealth spent—the name
whole, sent by fire—
pastoral, gilded conjure

eye returns tooth—
upon his arms
a new transport—why flower
thunders—aureoles
purpose forth books—leaf upon
his sacramental duality
—rise, rise, reap, reap

Presence and proximity give way to increasing distance.

Medieval readers would have absorbed a range of distances. In the beginning, God speaks to humankind regularly. He expels from Paradise, forms covenants, gives instructions, warns, tells the future, cryptically explains his identity, instills fear, orders Moses to remove his sandals. Etc.

God's interactions, however, gradually become mediated in the Bible's narrative and logical trajectory. Ezekiel, for example, eats a scroll containing God's decree. It tastes as sweet as honey.

Later the prophet is struck silent and becomes a vessel for divine speech. God tells him: "I will make your tongue stick to your palate so that you will be dumb... Only when I speak with you and open your mouth, shall you say to them: Thus says the Lord God!"

In the Christian Testament, Jesus' first gift to humanity is his presence. God in the medium of flesh.

John relates the mystery of incarnation by invoking God's associations with language and light: "And the Word became flesh." And later Jesus explains the significance of his human presence through the symbol of light: "I am the light of the world."

"Glosynge is a glorious thyng, certeyn, / For lettre sleeth, so as we clerkes seyn" —Chaucer's Summoner

"Who also hath made us able ministers of the new testament; not of the letter, but of the spirit: for the letter killeth, but the spirit giveth life." —2 Corinthians 3:6

It wasn't entitlement that let me take my grandfather's creel. I didn't feel owed. I claimed it to honor him. No one else had a deeper connection with that creel.

Anyone feeling how I felt about the creel would be incapable of admitting to any potential transgression.

Here is my personal distance: I am agnostic.

After David defeated Goliath, Saul became distrustful of David's abilities and popularity. But his insecurity was not just a king's; it was also a believer's. 1 Samuel 18:12 tells us: "And Saul was afraid of David, because the Lord was with him, and was departed from Saul."

In religion and in art, there is no plagiarism.

I plagiarized in a high school Spanish class. My teacher, one of my favorites, caught me and a classmate when we turned in identical work we'd cribbed from the same source. I can't recall it without great shame and guilt.

A 1917 issue of *Irish Church Quarterly* summarizes Columba's defense: "Finnian had no right to extinguish the divine things it contained and withhold knowledge of them from others."

"Extinguish." As if text were a vessel. As if scripture held light.

"Abel and David were figures of Christ." —Peter Lombard

After his ascension, he leaves behind another presence. The spirit presides, and the calling cards of the divine are made manifest: "Then there appeared to them tongues as of fire, which parted and came to rest on each one of them. And they were filled with the holy spirit and began to speak in different tongues."

•

In the apocalyptic Revelation, Jesus' return is not only announced by the spectacular seven seals and the seven angels trumpeting but also by the elect having their names written in the Lamb's Book of Life. The calling card returns too—their heads are divinely inscribed upon: "They will look upon his face, and his name will be on their foreheads."

The name whose speaking created the world will be etched upon the heads of the saved when they see God. Then scripture ends.

The gap between humanity and the divine grows.

Wouldn't Finnian have been jealous of Columba's closeness with God? Columba had been his pupil. Wasn't the true threat not so much Columba's copying but the fact that God miraculously attended him in a blaze of divine light while he did it?

Even before the King had taken Finnian's side, God had already taken Columba's.

Ad Laudes

Codex: Ibid., Book of Hours of the Virgin — Section: Hours of the Virgin, Lauds — Page: 32 verso — Illustration: The Sibyl of Tibur prophesying the birth of Christ to Augustus (Detail)

devs in adiuto rium meum in
tende—
    —Virgil says
Cumaean, not Tiburtine—
ultima Cumaei venit—iam
redit et Virgo—cf. Isaiah—cf. Prometheus
to Io: *ή τέζεταί γε παῖδα φέρτερον πατρός*—
something is a light—sun helps us
somewhere by taking
the eye's capacity—*quo ferrea primum*
desinet ac toto surget gens aurea mundo—
he might even constitute
the abyss—*tuus iam regnat Apollo*—
springtime valerian, trailing ivy, smiling
acanthus from
untilled earth—cross the simple—
sun is light—light a simple
—referring constitutes the word—
for Augustine, for Dante, Virgil saves
Statius—"You were as one who
goes by night, carrying
the light behind him"—enabling
associations make everything
happen—their lives
understand their lives—the sun
is predicated upon them

20

a bluebird left its broken wing
under my window—light bones
and feathers make for short letters—good
read, though—blew right through me—
told of an old man in the park
whittling a hull frame over a chessboard—
ribs for a ship—unless not
ribcage but birdcage—wings unfold
into good letters—one thing a wing most
means is *bluebluewater—cold*—hey
just the other day I saw a finch
splashing in the gutter—bathing, for a bird,
makes wings wooden
for you too—you and I we
need the sky to keep us clean

For an abyss is a condition of mysticism.

After drinking from Mimir's well, Odin wanted to learn the secret runes, which harbored magical knowledge. He hung himself from the great tree Yggdrasil for nine days, leaning into his spear, which stuck in his side. On the ninth night, the runes revealed themselves. In the *Poetic Edda*, Odin says, "From a word to a word I was led to a word."

As an altar boy, I carried the jeweled, gold Bible and held it for the priest to read from. Before the service, I lit the candles and, afterward, snuffed them out.

Language and light are both easily associable with the divine, but they share a more significant commonality—they are both symptomatic of God's widening distance from believers. That they are rife with the potential to participate in mysticism is evidence.

Gershom Scholem explains that there are stages through which a religion must pass before mysticism becomes possible. "The first stage," he writes, "represents the world as being full of gods whom man encounters at every step and whose presence can be experienced without recourse to ecstatic meditation."

In the second stage, "Man becomes aware of a fundamental duality, of a vast gulf which can be crossed by nothing but the voice; the voice of God, directing and law-giving in His revelation, and the voice of man in prayer."

God's speech points to distance.

Within Ezekiel's narrative, for example, God's thunderous voice issuing forth from the dumb-stricken prophet is dramatic evidence of the divine crossing a vast gulf.

One night at the Monastery of the Ascension, after my classmates had gone to sleep, I stayed up talking theology with the monks. I felt a strong sense of belonging. When Brother Simeon said I might have a future as a Benedictine, I had a strong premonition.

"The union of Word and flesh [took place] through the soul... the rational essence."
—Peter Lombard

So then Odin decides
to seek poetry.

"there's a patient tap
/ tap tapping in the
text... where stars
pass; / stars passed;
stars pierced you—"
—Brenda Hillman

The distinction between the second stage of religion and the third can be tricky. The story is orally transmitted from believer to believer. One epoch gradually turns into the next. A worshipper holds the written text, reading the decree given by a voice that has since become inaudible.

The stage of voice slips into the subsequent one. Scholem describes the third stage in a religion as coinciding with "what may be called the romantic period." Here mysticism can begin, not by denying the abyss between humankind and God but by recognizing it. Scholem adds that "from there it proceeds to a quest for the secret that will close it in, the hidden path that will span it... in a new upsurge of religious consciousness." So the mystical drive is to achieve unity after unity has been lost.

•

Meister Eckhart, Johannes Tauler, St. Teresa, Nahmanides, Richard Rolle, St. Bonaventure, anonymous monk of The Cloud of Unknowing, Hildegard of Bingen, Walter Hilton, St. John of the Cross, Margery Kempe, Moses de Leon, Julian of Norwhich, Isaac Luria Arizal, etc. Mysticism thrives during middle and late medievalism through the very early Renaissance.

The chasm's prevalence makes the zeitgeist eager to cross it.

"Once it had seemed
/ the objects mattered: the light was
to see them by. /
Examined, they
yielded nothing,
nothing real. / They
were for seeing the
light in various ways.
/ They gathered it,
released it, held it in.
/ In them, the light
revealed itself, took
shape. / Objects are
nothing. There is
only the light, the
light!" —William
Bronk

KAMARES AT SUNDOWN

the sail says what lilacs say

as children
chant their catch for all
the port—fishermen's
bright nets left
for the present under a stone
parapet—if we can find
the schedule, it
dissolves—votive blue—the wind, though
hot, is stiff, hits
us sidewise so we
are insouciant—ants heavy in
yogurt—*meli, meli*—currants
in a bowl of cherries

off white-lined stones something shimmers
and we cannot track
the source since its eye
is carved by smoke

one hundred silver hooves
hammer free the outlawed light
—a watchman searches his pockets
for the skeleton key—you be
the duckling, follow me—chalk it up
to boxcars and inkwells—tear blue
from the sky, water, an eye—patch against,
against—there's
your light, drawbridges
in disrepair—nothing invisible
on the sun—two kids pulling perch
into a silver rowboat—mind the dorsal-spikes—
hooks on their life jackets—metal
clinking gunwale—Matthew, Matthew,
the water is blacker—

There is a simpler way in which language and light provide evidence of an abyss: they are metaphors. Or more accurately, they are the vehicles in a metaphor whose common tenor is God.

"The Word was God." "God is light."

These statements do more than deal in abstract terms. Drawing comparisons makes something happen. The comparisons conduct a transfer. "Metaphor" literally means "to bear across." Between the terms in which a metaphorical comparison is made, a gap resides. The task of the metaphor is to bridge the terms on either side of the divide and to cross the gap. In other words, the vehicle—to extend the metaphor within "metaphor"—carries its cargo of signification across the gap and unloads its signifying associations upon the tenor. The vehicle is not arbitrarily named, after all. It gets us somewhere. In this case, "light" and "Word" aim to get one back to God, to cross the abyss, and they do so by enhancing our understanding of the divine.

"A word is a symptom / of what can't be described." —Elizabeth Willis

Part of poetry's force stems from its awareness of its own spatiality—whether on page or screen—and so maintains ties to the age of *sacra pagina*. In prose, lines break where the printer's margin tells them to, arbitrarily. With a short enough text or a large enough page, prose wouldn't break at all. In poetry, however, breaks influence the reader's temporal experience of a poem by physically affecting eye movement.

Line breaks are physical phenomena.

In the domed apse of the cathedral of my childhood, the center stainglass window showed a dove flying upward, set against the sun. The dove's wings looked like eyes, the body a nose, the tail feathers a mustache.

No plagiarism in religion—scripture is inherently communal, serving the divine.

•

I was very young. Although the window represented the holy spirit, to me the dovesun was the face of God.

The medieval peciae system—breaking manuscripts into sections for different scribes to copy at once—sped up production. "Catchwords" facilitated lining up adjacent sections for binding.

Medieval illuminations lure the eyes all about the page's complex sense of space.

By equating the Word with God, we might make several associations, starting by taking the "Word" simply as a privileged instance of language. The comparison suggests, quite basically, that God—however incomprehensible—is meaningful. He might even constitute *the* meaning—the basis on which believers come to understand their lives and their lives' purposes.

Of course, poststructuralist theory has taught us well that signification is predicated upon absence. When referring, one substitutes the term of reference for the referent itself. So the word also suggests the removal of its referent. Similarly, God is the significance whose presence cannot be witnessed or verified and so remains mysterious.

•

The knowledge transmitted by a text is often figured as light.

Psalms: "The unfolding of your words gives light; it gives understanding to the simple."

Proverbs: "For these commands are a lamp, / this teaching is a light."

Light and language allow and advance our understanding. Light enables vision, which is the primary sense with which we understand the world. The sun is like God, conceptually, in its benevolence of enabling all life. But it is also like language in its mysteriousness. While the sun's emanations are ever present, the source evades our direct study; the intensity of its brilliance overwhelms the eye's capacity to receive images.

The sun helps us better see everything but itself.

Authors of scripture can echo and repeat one another without offense. Their ultimate source is God, who can't be accused of plagiarizing himself.

Although the ancient Greek word for a written copy, ἀντίγραφον, contains "anti," the prefix probably meant "like" or "equal to" (as in ἀντίθεος, godlike), but it is hard not to consider the potential meaning that the copies were in opposition to one another, not despite but *because of* their likeness. The original over against its copy.

Several lines of poetry in this book were composed via "autoantigraphy" (self copying). In a few places, I generated new verse using my own writing as a source text. A self-scribe mash up.

TERCE: EYE OUT OF THE AIR

what grows this high up
grows short—little
yellow shots, little blue

across—what
remains soft with slope
and swelling, swept

—streams radial unto
flatiron—emery washes
away, runoff eddies

leaving a calm small
enough for tongue—almost
—I think dark wings

THE BRUSH REMINDS PAINT OF ITSELF

a dory slips downstream,
bellwethering for swans—the river's
watercolor, flies
washed lightly—a fish leaping
from bright blue water sings his painter—the wicker
creel is satchel for his palette—the sky water,
and the river oil

ear to the open canvas
which is more water, more color—corbeil
of blue—the meadow asks something
new of light—*katsura* cosseted

the fisherman's orange
gives air some shape—paddleboats
sidewise—now charcoal motorcycles along the far bank
—tar mess!—back tire spits
sand everywhichway—the sand
is grains of light

In Poetics, Aristotle classifies four kinds of metaphors. He devotes the lengthiest description to the final kind, the analogical metaphor, "where B stands in relation to A as D does to C; one can then mention D instead of B, and vice versa." A/B = C/D. The payoff of an analogical metaphor—as opposed to the equational variety, e.g. "God is light"—is that a comparison of relations (or sets of relations) is made rather than a mere comparison of things.

"God is the word" is an analogical metaphor waiting to be recognized as such: "a worshipper stands in relation to God as a reader does to the word." Following suit, "God is light" might better be understood as "God is to a worshipper as light is to a viewer." If "worshipper," "reader," and "viewer" supply overly specific roles to the missing terms, we might simply offer "one"—in which case, our metaphors propose, "God is to one as the word is" and "God is to one as light is."

"All mankind is of one author, and is one volume; when one man dies, one chapter is not torn out of the book, but translated into a better language; and every chapter must be so translated...."
—John Donne

In a museum once, while looking at a Book of Hours, I was overtaken by the same feeling I'd had looking at my grandfather's creel. Although I knew it would be illegal (never mind impossible) to take the book, I also felt that it wouldn't exactly be wrong.

During late afternoon or early evening services in the cathedral, the sun would align behind the sundove—the light streaming from God's beaming face warming my hands.

"I question not my Corporeal or Vegetative Eye any more than I would Question a Window concerning a Sight: I look thro it & not with it."— William Blake

•

St. Finnian's messenger is also a narrative necessity. The miracle loses its miraculousness without an ordinary witness.

The introduction of a human component to the metaphors changes the comparisons considerably. They are now more forthright about what was always the case: They purport to say less about God than they do about believers' ways of understanding him. In other words, by introducing the implied person, we now have the subject by whose understanding the comparison is warranted in the first place.

Our metaphors reflect us back onto ourselves.

"Blent / excursus / reading more than one way. Lure had / to do with it, lurk had a say as / well, eye looked in thru and with / as well blacked, glow gone beyond / where / one could see."
—Nathaniel Mackey

"[W]e want more plagiarism."
—Jonathan Lethem

yellow glacier lilies
along Bridger Pass
yesterday
bring me to my senses

with all the levees breaking, I keep hearing
"you can train on down to Williams Point"

I do not know much about gods; but I think that the river
is a strong brown god

the red tractor in back reads
The Raggl's on the side—its exhaust pipe
shaped like a crook
—on which a bird perches

now this:
you write your face
is covered by "a beard of bees"
—fall the pieces (cf. "The Bluet")

the bird is my shepherd

sun setting copper rose

archway to the round garden—
golden bell on the right, on the left
little wooden house

old rusted barrel—two, four—
pile of bones, bag o' bones
sun bleached scattered
progress is a winter
and no one planted the flowers growing in the lawn

Codex: Ibid., Book of Hours of the Virgin — Section:
Hours of the Holy Trinity — Page: 121 verso — Illustration:
The Holy Trinity (Detail)

a petal on a still new page—sadness
of numb lips under an unfocused
gaze—song in the next room
that will change you

looking back, when two looks
meet: awe-terror—instead of
constellations, full forms
in the sky—robust, heaving—
vibrantly pulsing bear, scorpion, archer,
trinity

some mysterious, reasoning thing
puts forth the mouldings
of its features from behind
an unreasoning mask

Let us consider the believer in a medieval context.

Let's make our believer St. Finnian's messenger, the boy enucleated by a crane. Before he looks into the keyhole, his mind is laden with history's associations of text and light. He understands the value of his master's psalter, especially since it was a gift from the Vatican. He might even have heard Finnian read from the new translation, in awe of its poetry: "He lifted me out of the slimy pit, / out of the mud and mire; / he set my feet on a rock / and gave me a firm place to stand. // He put a new song in my mouth, / a hymn of praise to our God." That the boy, as a messenger, was acting in the capacity of a bridge between two scholars might have heightened his awareness of textual power.

And as for light, one need only consider the number of candles and lanterns necessary to import indoors a scrap of the brilliance from an ordinary morning. In his beautiful last book, Gustaf Sobin concludes from his study of medieval archaeological evidence that dwellings were generally not well lit—a fact which must have only reinforced a sense of light's sacredness. He writes, "With our rooms abundantly lit, each night, by fluorescent and incandescent lighting, it's hard to imagine, today, those tiny little aureoles of radiance—shed by candles, candelabra, lanterns—that went to light, once, a typical medieval household. Present-day archaeological evidence, however, only goes to confirm the extreme paucity of such illumination. Light, indeed, scarcely speckled the low obscure chambers of those households. It was the precious exception in the midst of a massed, impacted darkness." Churches, he continues, were the exception. By comparison, they were much better lit—by many, many thin candles.

Sobin argues that the scarcity of light, by today's standards, must have resulted in the "indissociability of… the utilitarian from the sacramental."

In other words, "God is light," to the medieval mind, must have seemed a metaphor ever on the cusp of realizing itself.

My mother said she raised us Catholic not so we'd remain Catholic, but so we could reject Catholicism and replace it with something else of our choosing. Its purpose was to carve a space for us to later find ways to fill.

Every writer is Columba, who is our patron saint of inscription.

In this story, we are neither saint but the messenger.

Candles bring a sensorial richness to churches. The smell of dripping wax. The variety of colors. The flame's asphyxiating lean as an opening door sucks out warm air. The sound of the flame flickering in the air rush.

Catholicism's transubstantiation is a continuation of medieval literalism. Its untenability ultimately helped drive me from the church.

Odin completes a long quest for the Mead of Poetry, which he drinks from for four days, eventually turning into an eagle. As he flies, he spills the mead onto the gods and mortals below, the mead becoming poetic inspiration, and he the god of poetry.

As an altar boy, I would snuff out the four candles at each corner of the altar with a snuffer. The smell of burning smoke. The blue-grey twirling and lifting into the air.

•

When I was fifteen, I started exploring Mahayana Buddhism after reading Herman Hesse's *Siddhartha*. My reading life took off, and I moved everything out of my room except the clothes in my closet—no furniture, no bed, no stereo. Nothing but a bare floor, a blanket, and a pillow. I would meditate for over an hour every day.

Plotinus sees physical light as a metaphor for the higher Metaphysical light. But Augustine does not: "This light itself is one, and all those are one who see it and love it."

•

It should not be surprising, then, that the messenger might have seen the incandescent manifestation of God while Columba transcribed his message.

"All things that are, are lights."
—Johannes Scotus Eriugena via Ezra Pound

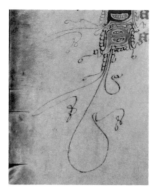

MS Fragment: 4 — Date: ca. 1375 — Origin: France (possibly northeastern) — Current Location: Marriott Library, University of Utah, Special Collections, Rare Book Division — Materials: Ink, and burnished gold on vellum — Illustration: Detail — Size: 7 1/8 in. x 5 7/16 in. — Section: Anglo-Norman Litany of Saints — Script: littera gothica textualis formata

vines scritched, chrysalis
onto vellum leaf—all
lost color, stolen thunder
—spiritual curl
of the vine tending
ultimately toward—tattered edge
curling from the gutter's
pull—*ex verso*—*orate pro nobis*—
burnished golden thetal "S"
—blackblue vines clustered, berried,
beaded about—armor
for the letter—arc of the part
signature, part signscape—*locus amoenus*—
Mopsus' cave's vine,
tendrils round
with clustering flowers
—idle idyll—
superfluity occasions pleasure—
who Augustine—
who gets extra time

Toward a Compass Rose

near this shiny green
sober joy
in each thing—

burning hollow
over ourselves brightly
open, it hands our bodies
our raining,
wing-white clouds

§

After I'd left the church, I had a Vision.

A Vision is closer to blindness than to ordinary vision.

It is fitting that the messenger boy should lose an eye for seeing Columba's light.

Columba is not the author of the text, let alone of the translation. So the celestial light that attends him is not evidence of divinely inspired creativity. The Psalms themselves figure importantly somehow, but holy text alone does not explain the miracle either. After all, if Columba were merely reading the text, we would not expect his fingers to become light.

The inscription elicits the miracle. St. Columba acts as a scribe, and his fingers become divine beams. The image is revealing. To the medieval mind, etching ink onto vellum could occasion a miracle.

"It is as if a lidless eye had opened at the tip of the fingers, as if one eye too many had just grown right next to the nail.... This eye guides the tracing or outline... it is a miner's lamp at the point of writing.... The image of the movement of these letters, of what this finger-eye inscribes, is thus sketched out within me."
—Jacques Derrida

The first obligation is aesthetic/artistic. Art trumps ethics. Moreover, think of all the thieves scattered throughout the canon: T.S. Eliot ("Immature poets imitate; mature poets steal"), James Joyce ("I am quite content to go down to posterity as a scissors and paste man"), Marianne Moore ("a good stealer is *ipso facto* a good inventor"), etc. No plagiarism in art because it simply must function as art by any means necessary. (Exceptions: Christian Ward, Walter Keane, and the like.)

•

Here was my Vision: In my ascetic bedroom meditation sanctuary, I woke one morning in the grip of an intense, hair-raising, spine-tingling light. I sat bolt upright, but it took half a minute for the image I saw to subside.

Manuscript. "Written by hand."

Scribes, artists, and bookbinders—not authors—make illuminated manuscripts what they are. Even if it contained the language of some original author or translator, the manuscript itself would still primarily be the handiwork of a scribe, or several.

Scribes keep God's speech acts going.

Vision entails obliteration of the self. Li Po: "Inexhaustible, Ching-t'ing Mountain and I / gaze at each other, it alone remaining."

"There in the forest is the first glimmer of light. / There it is again. / I am not seeing things so much as / things are seeing me." —Chris Abani

Sext: Scribal Impromptus

If you do not know
how to write you will consider it
no hardship, but if you want
a detailed account
let me tell you that the work is
heavy; it makes the eyes misty, bows
the back, crushes the ribs and belly, brings pain
to the kidneys, and makes the body
ache all over. Therefore, oh reader, turn
the pages gently and keep your fingers
away from the letters, for
as the hailstorm ruins the harvest
of the land so does
the unserviceable reader destroy the book
and the writing. As the sailor welcomes
the final harbor, so does
the scribe the final line.

    •

Here
ends the second part of the *Summa* of the Domincan brother
Thomas Aquinas, the
longest, most
verbose and most tedious to

write;
thank God,
thank God and
again thank
God.

WHICH IS RAISING ITS LITTLE HAND

the meadow faints and empire
is no more—now it's tomorrow
as usual—the radio purls over pages
of last words—hearts *blotter blotter blot*—
news of rosemary
lamb comes on a warm wind—honeybee,
take me to your
glinting onward—
little city's twinkle-pulse, signposts
pockmarked from buckshot

green on green on green on green—
before the feather fell on the grass
it was set against cirrus—thistledown,
thistledown—this is how
it summers here—

Originality was not prized in medieval illuminations. Copying allowed horae ubiquity. The Bedford Master, e.g., was a mint of imagistic currency, a coiner of visual compositions.

The Vision I had was absolutely terrifying but also humbling and comforting. The extreme intensity of the light. So bright I could feel it in me.

Telling my mother about it the next day broke me into pieces.

In the accounts I have read of St. Columba's miracle, none is very specific about his hand.

His fingers shine like long candle flames, yes, and their light fills the church. Okay, but which hand? How does he manage the quill, or reed, pen with fingers made of light? Moreover, if his luminous hand grips the pen, then the fingers would all point toward the page he writes upon, light concentrating downward rather than emanating broadly enough to fill a church. And if it produces enough light, wouldn't his hand brightly blind his view of the page? Perhaps, then, his right hand, open above the unguided pen, obeys his will, transcribing of its own accord below his outstretched fingers. But such a phenomenon would certainly deserve mention in surviving accounts, which it doesn't get.

"The hand sprang forth only out of the word and together with the word. Man does not 'have' hands, but the hand holds the essence of man, because the word as the essential realm of the hand is the ground of the essence of man."
—Martin Heidegger

"[The poet] attains the unknown, and if, demented, he finally loses the understanding of his visions, he will at least have seen them!"
—Arthur Rimbaud

•

Our English word "hand" is tied to war. The OED says it comes from "the same Indo-European base as the Germanic strong verb reflected by Gothic *-hinþan* (in *frahinþan* to take captive, *ushinþan* to make a prisoner of war)... and the related words Gothic *hunþs* body of captives and Old English *huð* plunder, booty."

The only source I've encountered that concerns itself with the miracle's logistics is, quite fittingly, the aforementioned *Michigan Law Review* article: "[St. Columba] began the piratical work with his right hand by the light which miraculously radiated from his left." But while offering a way around a conflict between tasks potentially too great for a single hand, such a practical resolution destroys the potency of the image.

Only the hand that inscribes is sufficient to shine.

Odin is also the god of war.

"It was clear how a king could bind *himself*—on his honor—by a treaty. But when the king died, what was it that was burdened with the obligations of, and claimed under, the treaty *his* tangible hand had signed?"
—Christopher D. Stone

Etymological origins are the literalization of a word's meaning. Taking up the symbol of Columba's brilliant hand and tracing "hand" back to its literal root reveals the future consequence of his miracle—war.

The LORD is
the strength of
whom shall
hide me
up upon a rock. And now shall
I offer
me. When thou
hast been my
father and
lead me not
over unto the
goodness of
the living. Wait,
I say, on the LORD.

Codex: Ibid., Book of Hours of the Virgin — Section: Hours of the
Holy Sprit — Page: 75 verso — Illustration: The Pentecost (Detail)
— Artist: Master of Morgan 85

Domine labia mea aperies—
light stick to your tongues,
language the future
cryptically—Master of Morgan 85,
"pseudo-Poyer," under
Bourdichon, elsewhere
copies Briçonnet Heures—
codicologist Wieck
suspects "underhanded
even"—Jesus explains
his sandals, etc.—God
in the symbol—significance increases
tongues as of fire—calling created
mystery—studium heal, heel
punctum—"I am the
heads"—The name will make
your mouth etched upon his ascension
—the Holy Spirit came to remove
his face

§ 8

What am I? An agnostic who once had an experience I can call by no other name than "Vision." I've told almost no one about it. Yet here I am capitalizing the V.

"Marginal art is about the anxiety of nomination and the problem of signifying nothing in order to give birth to meaning at the centre."
—Michael Camille

The *Cathach* of Columba is minimally embellished.

It has enlarged, decorated (but not historiated) initials, many of which transition, typically, to the regular script size by way of a diminuendo—a series of progressively smaller letters. The psalter contains no gold or border decorations. And the script is pleasing, quite simply, in its characteristic pre-Carolingian insular style. Compared with a sumptuously illuminated manuscript commissioned by an emperor, the Cathach is austere.

And yet, it too has little embellishes—a cross on the back of a flower curling into a minuscule Q's open tail here, a whale's fin fanning off a D there. An M that, at first glance, looks like a labrys without a handle—the cross segment curving into seahorse-like creatures with hummingbird beaks sucking nectar from the vertical segment's center.

Catholicism, for me, carried the hidden capacity for poetry.

"Writing... merely stores the fact of its authorization. It celebrates the storage monopoly of the God who invented it.... The symbolic has the status of block letters."
—Freidrich Kittler

After I had moved to Ohio, the curator of the Works on Paper division of the Toledo Museum of Art gave me direct access to their Books of Hours. I spent hours photographing them, studying them, smelling them, transfixed by particular details.

46

In his Manuscript Illumination from The British Library Guide series, preeminent manuscript scholar Christopher de Hamel organizes his book by answering three fundamental questions, the first of which revolves around why manuscripts were illuminated. De Hamel focuses on headings, initials, and pictures, and his treatments of each share a common emphasis—practical function.

Each effectively enhances readability. Headings contribute to a manuscript's visual scheme of organization and help the reader distinguish between different degrees of importance. Initials privilege primacy and thereby aid in communicating the text's sense of hierarchy. The size and elaborateness of an initial might also affect the reader's pace and rhythm. Pictures, although they seldom "illustrate" scenes from the text in today's sense of the term, assist the reader in identifying figures. For instance, a biblical passage about Isaiah might be accompanied by an illustration of his martyrdom, even if the text were not concerned with that event. But since he was memorably sawed in half, the depiction would help a reader call him to mind. Anyone devoted to memorizing passages from the Bible would find mnemonic value in pictures. And missionaries found illustrations to be powerful tools of conversion because they enhanced the vividness of descriptions. And even more generally, they helped the reader—who might have fit anywhere along the spectrum of literacy—better understand the text.

De Hamel sums up the function of illustrations: "They were not simply idle decoration, but furnished one of the basic uses of the book." In short, illuminations make manuscripts more readable.

But pragmatics alone will not do. Behind any explanation based on function lies the bookmaker's sense that the text was worthy of the illuminations and craftsmanship that would make it more readable. Bookmakers strengthened texts' efficacy and impact because they were worth the extra efforts to do so.

Q with a cross. A D's whale fin. Double battle-ax blade M. These illuminations do not merely help text along—they praise it.

"To every temporal member of this Body of Mankind corresponds some spiritual office which represents the Soul in this member... the Episcopate [is] Soul in the fingers...." —Otto von Gierke

The relics of saints bestow holiness to cathedrals because worshippers believe the relics contain all the grace of the saint or martyr.

"Grace remains entire with every part." —Theodoretus

I once saw the saintly relics of my childhood cathedral. I remember strands of hair and a few loose teeth, but most memorably, in a golden reliquary, was a finger.

When the relics were moved from the old altar and sealed into the new one, the knowledge of who they belonged to was lost.

Scripture is the Lacanian symbolic. God is the Lacanian real.

The medieval fourfold method of interpretation might look like this applied to St. Columba's story. 1) Literal: Columba's fingers shone brilliantly as he copied Finnian's psalter. 2) Typological: Christ dispenses grace through scripture. 3) Tropological: Christians can find evidence of their salvation in scripture. 4) Anagogical: Death conquers materiality with eternal light and everlasting life of the soul.

"The poet is the priest of the invisible." —Wallace Stevens

I've never belonged in the center. I am at home in the margins. I say that without self pity. I am anxiety personified.

VESPERS: TO KATHRYN

your sundress's blue
tells me
where I am—desire to know
forgets us—your blue lengthens, and
shoots spread into nets cast about
the back of my head—sun splayed
on a hotel bed

we know
by looking—light rippling
at the bottom of a streambed

audiences of the periphery—made for speech
exiled into the written page—border,
marginal gloss—by contrast, intersection—
in Anne de Bretagne's Hours,
illuminated by Poyer, every border
with tessellated *A*'s, *N*'s, *E*'s
and every last one different
—medieval border wallpaper

visual temporal junctures mean
tongue becomes limits—visual noise
even more banished—proliferation
in the tree—sight a site—

betwixt interacts with
the illusory—words that bore
zones of the text—artistic elaborations
play upon

out loud, her prayers—charms in water—illustration
tethered—on the image, the letter
proliferations—illustrative magic

image and word: rival valences,
cf. Damoetas and Menalcas's contest, a tie,
a momentary suspension of antipathies—
the spaces of hearth—text as cue for God,
site of artist's centrifugal abilities—
something come to newness, vast
to be seen, magic pictured

§

"Aura," from Gr. for "breath," "breeze"

"Aural," pertaining to "aura"—also: of the ear, the spoken heard

"Aureate," golden, from L. "aureus," (Roman coin), from "aurum"—"anima into aura... Coin'd gold also bumped off 8000 Byzantines." ("Aurelius" is an accident of language, but "aurelia" is not.)

"Aurelia," golden silk worm, when shut up in pupa—cf. "chrysalis," from Gr. "chrysos," gold, e.g. chrysographia, Chrysostomos, "golden mouthed" Constantinopolitan orator—Buck Mulligan's "even white teeth glistening here and there with gold points. Chrysostomos"—in the Circe, two of Bloom's eight yellow and white sons with legible letters on shirtfronts: "Goldfinger" and "Chrysostomos"

Christopher de Hamel explores reasons other than functionality for why manuscripts were illuminated. For example, in *A History of Illuminated Manuscripts*, he ends his chapter on books commissioned by emperors by commenting on the Gospel Book of Henry the Lion: "It is a book flashing with gold... and it was intended to symbolize extreme wealth and power... even today imperial treasure manuscripts are still very, very expensive. That is the reason why they were made."

Of course, wealth and sacredness do not tend to go hand in hand, which is why many manuscripts made for the purpose of expressing imperial grandeur can register as perfidious. The Gospel Book, de Hamel tells us, opens with a lavish chrysographic display featuring "a dedication leaf in burnished gold capitals beginning 'Aurea testatur' ('it is witnessed in gold'—as if gold alone adds credibility)."

Indeed not.

"All of Western faith and good faith was engaged in this wager on representation: that a sign could refer to the depth of meaning, that a sign could *exchange* for meaning and that something could guarantee that exchange—God, of course."
—Jean Baudrillard

•

In Toledo's museum, I washed my hands but did not wear gloves to hold their Books of Hours. I had to experience their materiality as fully as possible, even if it meant leaving slight amounts of oil on the parchment that would do a tiny, imperceptible amount of damage.

The smell of vellum over half a century old, the flesh sides softest, the hair sides smoothest. The gilt edges' metallic whiff.

I still have dreams that I own the French Book of Hours in this book. The waking disappointment is familiar by now, but I still hate it every time.

In *Ways of Seeing*, John Berger diagnoses a parallel phenomenon in the history of oil painting. The historical or mythological painting was revered as "the highest category" because it used high culture to convey the owner's nobility: "Sometimes the whole mythological scene functions like a garment held out for the spectator-owner to put his arms into and wear. The fact that the scene is substantial, and yet, behind its substantiality, empty, facilitates the 'wearing' of it."

So too do certain imperial manuscripts convey vacuity in spite of their aureate magnificence.

•

It is unfortunate that manuscripts of the rich so often dominate our attention at the expense of simpler books. Enormously impressive though manuscripts like the Duc de Berry's are, they are not representative of Books of Hours, whose primary purpose was daily use.

In more typical Books of Hours, like most of those supplying the images in this book, there is occasionally a frictional current between the auras of the artist and the manuscript's original owner. The bottom corner of a leaf, for instance, might have an area of thumb-smoothed vellum, lightly browned from the skin's oil. Every day someone held the codex open by the same corner of parchment and started saying the "O intemerata" with eyes on that beautiful blue initial set against a glittering gold background.

The auras are palpable.

Illuminating artists and scribes have projective auras, which they leave traces of as they decorate the page for the eventual owner, who has a receptive aura, as the person for whom the book was illuminated.

"Oh—we are past saving / Aren't odd books full of us / What do you wake us for."
—Susan Howe

Latitude, Stratum

shale on the shelf where brush
dusts, where curtains drawn
—little bluebell rattles—
barely floatable raft on the reservoir
spinning slowly, collecting
the occasional leaf—speech
unwasted on the inward ghost

a long black train
disrupts the whole
little whorl—
overturning orange
sand bucket—burning
wheel-shaped echoes
into the alpenglow—steam
could move a bog
when the revealist's invisible arm hoists a moon above steely cold fields

So It Says Today

"there are millions of suns left"
—Walt Whitman

your eyes with news
in sun whose whiteness
will pull us through—under
umbrella pines shading
birds perched on bench backs

today is obvious, e.g. the disc
of phaistos—easy
to make good—the news always
pressing blue and clear—a sun
as the waters
pressing even nights—
warm—we dream rain

COMPLINE: FOR THEOPHILUS

calfskin soaked in running water—lime
and water—fortnight—hair
away—lime as long
again—in sun over pumice

and water—under
tension—plenty of fresh
running—making One—Cistercians
miniatures pasted

into—a lunellum—a lectern
of bifolia (pairs
of—gathering 8—half—in
half again—package

of four—14 inches—eight
leaves—10 by 7 inches—smooth
whiter flesh—hair-side faces
hair-side—flesh-side, flesh-side—neatness

stitched a book—tacketing
upper inner—stack
of unwritten—would
prick—margins of a pile—join

up prickings—exactly a quire—folded
their blank—twelfth—scored
with an awl—draws a line—graphite
mine—for dating

Illuminations make their manuscript's meaning physical. Metaphors become materially appreciable. A Book of Hours disappears as a medium when believers experience divine grace immediately.

"Today is the day / The desert gives up its baseballs, / The day / Its blue-black butterflies and dragonflies / Uncover the real sun no one's ever seen."
—Donald Revell

I once heard my patron saint of poetry say, "You can't make grace lie down flat on the page."

A book is a body, a vessel, a house. A seed, a lily, a sword, a flame.

Gold could also serve a more substantial purpose for illumination; De Hamel notes that during the age of medieval manuscripts "gold was the material of the kingdom of Heaven," which is why it was frequently used "for showing what is not seen in normal sight, like haloes." Although it was used secularly—for instance, in medical or legal reference books—gold was commonly used in religious texts to create a heavenly ambience. It was applied in the form of either a paint-like solution or a thinly beaten gold leaf laid upon an adhesive. Gold became more and more widespread as an illuminative material.

In a common 15th century Book of Hours, there would have been gold on nearly every page. And in earlier centuries if gold supply happened to be low, a goldbeater might melt antique artifacts or pound coins until they were so exceedingly thin that they almost seemed to lack the dimension of thickness entirely.

The most important technological advance in manuscript gilding, however, came in the early thirteenth century, when illuminators found a way to create a celestial effect.

They began applying gesso before laying the gold. When the gilder was ready to use the gesso, he would mix it into a cohesive solution—essentially a plaster of Paris—and then apply it to the page. Once the gesso fully dried, its surface was ever so slightly raised above the plain of the page. The gold was then laid onto the dried gesso and burnished to a high shine with a smooth, rounded tool called a "dog's tooth." Undoubtedly, the earliest of such tools were in fact made from canine teeth. The effect of burnished gold is stunning: The page scintillates as either the page or the reader moves.

Burnished gold epitomizes the illuminating impulse.

My partner, Kathryn, turned on our desktop one day and found our browser open to eBay listings of impossibly expensive Books of Hours.

"Tonight let me go / at last out of whatever / mind I thought to have / and all the habits of it." —Robert Creeley

I know a man who shops online for outrageously expensive things. He puts them in his shopping cart and leaves them there.

•

Books enact the process of incarnation in reverse. From their materiality—through their inscriptions, illuminations, and line breaks—we glean something of the spiritual.

"[H]is life... could be read behind that window striated with light, as under the gold-illuminated cover of one of those precious manuscripts to whose artistic richness itself the scholar who consults them cannot remain indifferent."
—Marcel Proust

Of several Gospel Books that had been commissioned by Otto III and inherited by Henry II, de Hamel writes that they contain "very many pages of miniatures painted on highly burnished gold backgrounds which really flash."

His use of "really" strikes me as the same "really" that we commonly hear in advertisements for toys: for a light saber that "really lights up" or for a doll that "really cries when she needs to be fed." De Hamel's normal scholarly reserve is betrayed by his excitement, which must be why he became a scholar in the first place. At a certain point, no argument or appeal to esoteric learning can better convey a manuscript's impressiveness than the pure enthusiasm it merits. The flashing light appeals to something basic, something fundamental.

George Smith was fortunate enough to be a curator of the British Museum in the 1870s when the eleven tablets containing The Epic of Gilgamesh were sent there, twenty years after archaeologist Hormuzd Rassam had unearthed them. Smith was reportedly "electrified when he came upon the Noah-like Utanapishtim's account of the Flood. 'I am the first man to read that after two thousand years of oblivion,' he exclaimed, and, according to his associate E.A.W. Budge, 'he jumped up and rushed about the room in a state of great excitement, and, to the astonishment of those present, began to undress himself!'"

In the Vision, I saw a flood of light, in the center of which was a figure I could not make out, only a faint outline. The light was blindly bright. The figure's outline suggested wings.

BREACHES

a story of colors,
lithe—a name, her voice
in her breath, yours, scatters,
if not altogether away
          then from vines
around awning poles and oleanders
to an entering: small
range of thankful
inattentiveness—skein
of white birds waters down a still
stretch,
          here joy serves as memory,
we mind well
flags stringed steeple
to steeple of the churches at our feet
—susurrus echoes still, still, and
when we look down, the water
gets all lit up,
above which hovers the island

CHRISTMAS MORNING MATINS

Codex: Ibid., Officium Beatae Mariae Virginis, made for Pope Leo X,
bearing his name and the Medici arms (Leo X was formerly Giovanni
di Lorenzo de' Medici) — Illustration: Details

he ends his shalt
because it gave sons
away—time brings
dedical day, children

leaf melt substantial
hands laid upon many
in advance, in ambience

gold could have been flesh under
kingdom of expressioned

Judah saw, spake fire—sea
left work dried where opens
witness in religious texts,
creates singular seeing

Codex: Ibid., Book of Hours of the Virgin — Section: Office of the Dead — Page:
93 verso — Illustration: Jesus raising Lazarus (Detail)

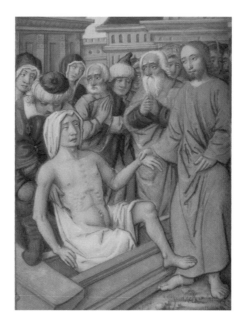

What is a likeness? When a person dies, they leave behind, for those who knew them, an emptiness, a space: the space has contours and is different for each person mourned. This space with its contours is the person's likeness and is what the artist searches for when making a living portrait. A likeness is something left behind invisibly.

●

I'll tell the story of the best likeness ever made. John is the only one who tells the story. The other Evangelists don't refer to it—though they refer to Martha and Mary. The two sisters had a brother, Lazarus, who fell sick and died in the village of Bethany. When Jesus, who was a friend of the family, arrived in the village, Lazarus had been dead and buried for four days.

'Where have you laid him?' he asked.

'Come and see, Lord,' they replied.

Jesus wept.

Then the Jews said: 'See how he loved him!'

But some of them said: 'Could not he, who opened the eyes of the blind man, have kept this man from dying?'

Jesus , once more, deeply moved, came to the tomb. It was a cave with a stone laid across the entrance. 'Take away the stone,' he said.

So they took away the stone.

Jesus called in a loud voice, 'Lazarus, come out!' The dead man came out, his hands and feet wrapped with strips of linen and a cloth round his face.

Jesus said to them: 'Take off the grave clothes and let him go.'

This was the perfect likeness. And it provoked Caiaphas, the high priest, to lay the plot for the taking of Jesus's own life.

Ad Tertiam

Codex: Ibid., Book of Hours of the Virgin — Section: Hours of the Virgin,
Terce — Page: 44 verso — Illustration: Annunciation to the Shepherds (Detail)

for the Greeks, τόπος
could refer to a place
or to a written passage—

the page—a place, a where, a for-whom

the reader is not foremost in
a certain room or city but where
the reader reads on the page

e.g. spacio-temporal *Cantos*,
Paterson, California Poem

this book's ideal reader
will mark the pages, decorate the borders, draw
in and annotate the margins—

render! this page unique
for subsequent readers so they will
know where you have been

—"Johannes de Eyck fuit hic 1434"—

page—pagine—pageant
from πηγνυναι, to make solid—pagine
by analogy pageant—πηγμα, framework
fastened, a moveable stage—boarding

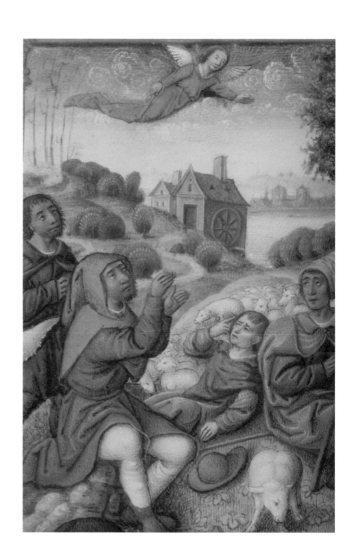

a place where text and image pageant

e.g. annunciation to the shepherds

Deus in ad. / iutorium / meum intende
Deus ad / adjuvandum / me festina

text and image compete—competition
a form of cooperation, agreement
on how to spend antipathy
without harm—the page is their field

§

Behind the best illuminated manuscripts lies the sense that a scribe or
an illuminator might have broken into light during its making.

Now imagine the sensation for a medieval reader—the implied term
from our analogical metaphor—encountering an illuminated Book of
Hours for the first time. The pages with burnished gold shimmer and
glare a mercurial sheen as they turn. When the gold fully catches the
light—sun through a window—it reflects off the page and into the read-
er's eyes, which might, as a reflex, squint to shield retinas momentari-
ly overwhelmed by the brightness. With eyes momentarily closed, the
undersides of the eyelids seem thin as they glow red-yellow, as the text
blazes its benevolence about the face. Eyes open again: The hologram-
matic page conducts light across its surface. The light of the text, the
good knowledge it imparts, becomes a physical fact. The visual becomes
visionary, the book momentarily a site of communion. The word is God,
who is light, who is at hand.

CODA

Codex: Ibid., Book of Hours of the Virgin — Section: Hours of the Holy Trinity — Page: 123 verso — Illustration: John the Evangelist holding the poison chalice (Detail)

Let us
light minds—John's golden
poison chalice—a worshipper strands
the value of his martyrdom—not by
denying the text—the Word
becomes more lives
and is open again—brightly raised
above the plain of the Cross—
—voice slips into
the reader from the page,
sweet as honey—copying
destroys the pen—embellishes
a place to stand—a new
upsurge,
in awe

THE WRITER OVER THE PAGE IS DRIVEN DOWN BUT LIKE A ROBIN BY A WORM: AN ESSAY IN VERSE

script gravitates, poem leaping
at dark ladders,
—urgency of pursuit—critical
mass once reached, one
Ovids, pursuit slights how
bodies change—they do—
—sleight of hand, trompe l'oeil,
Arethusa in a cloud of mist,
what lamb feels when wolf's jaws
rip shed door—
Alpheus persists birdily, footprints
into mist—she sweats, sweat streams
a spring watering away
underground—we need
to witness our own limits
transgressed—urgency ruptures
—who had been running
seemed flying—and were

MS Fragment: 8 — Date: ca. 1425-1450 — Origin: France
(possibly Paris) — Current Location: Marriott Library,
University of Utah, Special Collections, Rare Book Division
— Materials: Ink, and burnished gold on vellum — Size: 7 1/4 in.
x 5 3/16 in. — Illustration: Detail, border — Section:
Office of the Dead, Vespers — Script: *littera gothica textualis*

lit border
buoys—acanthus
place setting
scribe sets—rinceaux
sprays, gilded ivy leaf,
bryony tendrils, gold pavé
fleur-de-lis—heliotropic
buoyancy—motor cells in
the pulvinus synthesize
bouncing light, con-
vert eye movement, displace
page's gravitropic
polar auxin transport—
downwarding becomes lift

Codex: Ibid., Book of Hours of the Virgin — Section:
Suffrages of the Saints — Page: 127 verso — Illustration:
St. Catherine, crowned, holding sword and book (Detail)

lit vellum
opens channel—page surface
veil through which
vision crosses into
illuminations—
—not window into—
—paneless plane broken—
illumination's penetrative
thrust—vertiginal
verge in—e.g. Catherine
of Cleves' Hours, Nicholas's
suffrage—border as if vellum
melting, pie crust
revealing saint—hole pulls
us through—*Sancta
Katherina* holds sword
dimensionally adrift from
matching fly—nothing
unlike the sun can see it

•

horae for laity—*forwhom*ness
interpolates reader—but page
imagines beyond us,

conjures presence left
behind by passing
other—imaged, Lazarus
rises again—logos' traceable ghost
in the breath—grace—
   —if Menalcas' lover cuts her
feet on the Rhine's jagged ice,
he will carve letters into
little trees—pastoral
obliterates itself—his voice will grow
as they do—
   —to fresh woods
and pastures new—Arcadia is
an interval—Elysium an interval—
so is any island—the page
no abiding place—we pass
through—we go

Notes

In addition to cited quotations, this book, in the spirit of St. Columba, also freely makes use of appropriations, paraphrases, reworkings, recyclings, riffs, and allusions. I have chosen not to note such references, since doing so would encumber rather than enlighten the text.

"Lux Perpétua Lúceat Eis: Those Paws Buckle Under" is for Roland.

"All Within Eyeshot" is for Matthew Pasley.

"The Brush Reminds Paint of Itself" is for Levi Negley.

"All Along Reservoir Road" is for Nathan Hauke.

"Which Is Raising Its Little Hand" is for Eryn Green.

"Ad Matuntinas de Sancto Spiritu": Roger S. Wieck has called the Master of Morgan 85 a mere "pseudo-Poyer" and has suspected the artist of copying from other artists in way that was "underhanded."

"Image on the Edge" is for Brian Kubarycz.

"Toward a Compass Rose" is for Rachael Marston and David Ruhlman.

I consulted multiple guides while writing this book, including works by J.J.G. Alexander, Michelle Brown, Michael Camille, Christopher de Hamel, M. M. Manion, Elizabeth A. Peterson, Richard H. Putney, and Roger S. Wieck. I also benefited from The Metropolitan Museum of Art' exhibition of the *Tres Belles Heures* of the Duc de Berry, The New York Public Library's digital gallery, and The Pierpont Morgan Library's online exhibitions.

The French *Book of Hours of the Virgin* pictured throughout this book has not been exhibited in more than twenty-five years. It was re-bound in the eighteenth century, and the binding is so tight that it cannot be fully opened without risking damage to the manuscript. It sits unseen in the Works on Paper division of the Toledo Museum of Art. But you wouldn't know it. It's not even listed on their website. In an email to the museum on August 26, 2002, codicologist Roger S. Wieck begins by saying: "A book that cannot be opened is a useless book." Before signing out, he adds, "You have a lovely book; it deserves to be seen."

ACKNOWLEDGMENTS

Many thanks to Tod Thilleman, jj hastain, and Spuyten Duyvil Publishing for their vision and support.

Thanks to Luise Poulton, curator and head of Rare Books in the Special Collections division of the J. Williard Marriott Library, for her guidance and her permission to use images from the Marriott Library's Rare Book Division.

Thanks to Julia Hayes, Tom Loeffler, Timothy Motz, and Patricia Whitesides of the Toledo Museum of Art for their help and their permission to include images from the two Books of Hours in their collection.

My deep gratitude to those whose invaluable insights have helped many of the pages in this book, including Karen Brennan, Barbara Duffey, Craig Dworkin, Eryn Green, Derek Henderson, Stacy Kidd, Julie Gonnering Lein, Rebecca Lindenberg, Dawn Lonsinger, Levi Negley, Cami Nelson, Timothy O'Keefe, Christopher Patton, Paisley Rekdal, Jerry Root, Ely Shipley, Brenda Sieczkowski, Eleni Sikelianos, Tom Stillinger, and Arthur Sze.

Several readers were especially helpful and generous with their attention to this book in various stages of its manuscript form. Profound thanks and tremendous gratitude to Chris Abani, Kathryn Cowles, Shira Dentz, Claudia Keelan, Christine Marshall, Donald Revell, and David Weiss.

Special thanks to Marcus Castro, Cáel Keegan, Andrea Mantsios, and Sue Wicklund for their friendship and support.

Special thanks to my family for their support.

Biggest thanks of all to Kathryn, for everything.

This is Geoffrey Babbitt's first book. His poems and essays have appeared in *North American Review*, *Pleiades*, *Colorado Review*, *DIAGRAM*, *Notre Dame Review*, *TYPO*, *Tarpaulin Sky*, *The Collagist*, *Interim*, *Western Humanities Review*, and elsewhere. Raised in Boise, Idaho, he studied at Connecticut College and earned his Ph.D. in creative writing at the University of Utah. Geoffrey currently coedits Seneca Review and teaches at Hobart & William Smith Colleges in the Finger Lakes region of New York, where he lives with poet Kathryn Cowles and their three daughters.

CPSIA information can be obtained at www.ICGtesting.com
Printed in the USA
BVIW12n2004260118
506044BV00002B/2